Peter Cagney began his career in the service of laughter by contributing humorous material to newspapers and magazines and most of this material was world syndicated. Then he turned to the stage and broadcasting and he has written material for such noted artistes as Tommy Cooper, Ken Dodd, George Moon, Jimmy Logan, Bebe Daniels and Ben Lyon, Max Miller, to name only a few. Mr Cagney has written many novels including several thrillers, but his humorous books include, *Treasury of Wit and Humour*, *The Book of Wit and Humour* and *Current Comedy*.

Also in this series:

Edited by Peter Cagney

The Official Irish Joke Book No. 4

With additional material by Ernest Forbes
Illustrated by Lorne Brown

Futura

A Futura BOOK

First published in Great Britain by
Futura Publications Limited in 1979
Reprinted 1981, 1982, 1983, 1984

ISBN 0 7088 1646 0

Printed in Great Britain by
Hazell Watson & Viney Limited,
Member of the BPCC Group,
Aylesbury, Bucks

Futura Publications
A Division of
Macdonald & Co (Publishers) Ltd
Maxwell House
74 Worship Street
London EC2A 2EN
A BPCC plc Company

IRISH STREWTH

Dr Johnson always claimed that the Irish were a fair and truthful race of people with a tremendous ability to laugh at themselves and at the same time be incapable of speaking well of each other.

*   *   *

'God knows,' said Casey Milligan, 'that the best wits in the world are the Irish,' and to punch it home (which they do frequently), he quoted Swift, Sheridan, Wilde, Shaw and even Rafferty, the milkman.

*   *   *

The Dublin Opinion devoted many years to establishing the strength of Irish humour: and the best international comedy entertainers in the world include more than a few very humorous and lovable Irish stars.

*   *   *

The Irish people comprise a race which has never had to invent comedy. It is a natural asset.

*   *   *

Did you hear about the Irishman who thought that having it away was a football match?

* * *

Or the Irishman who thought that a bolt from the blue was running away from a police constable?

* * *

Or the Irish bird that killed itself with one stone? It was a hen trying to lay a 14 lb. egg.

* * *

Or the Irish archaeologist who thought that Ancient Tyre was a reject from a lorry's spare wheel?

* * *

Or the Irish zookeeper who thought that monkey business only went on in an apiary?

* * *

Or the Irishman so disenchanted with his wellies that he planted some shoe trees?

* * *

Or the Irish labourer who was so dumbfounded that he broke six fingers describing the foreman? And then complained that his wife didn't understand him? (And that goes for some of our readers!)

* * *

Or the Irishman who thought that 38–27–37 was the combination to his girlfriend's safe?

* * *

Or the Irishman who visited the doctor complaining of skin trouble because his wife wanted a mink coat?

* * *

Or the Irish teacher who thought that circling the square was the preoccupation of a mathematic street-woman?

* * *

Or the Irishman who complained of extravagant misuse of public money because the council permitted a zebra crossing in a street where he counted only three zebras over a period of three months?

* * *

Or the Irish pugilist who complained that the cock of the north had won by a foul?

* * *

Or the Irish sky-diver who went without a parachute and thought he was going to miss his target, but was only jumping to a conclusion?

* * *

Or the Irish BBC engineer who was given one of the highest posts in the organisation and told to erect it to provide the best signal? So he roped it to the flagstaff on Fenchstreet Station.

*　　*　　*

Or the Irish jewel thief who was born with a silver spoon in his mouth? Embossed with the Royal Arms in diamonds and emeralds.

*　　*　　*

Or the Irishman who bought his girl an expensive flared skirt for Christmas? The candles set it alight.

*　　*　　*

Or the girl who was supposed to meet the Irishman on the corner of Main Street. He asked her if she was Irish and she said, 'No, I'm Dorrish. Irish is in bed wis 'nother chap!'

*　　*　　*

Or the Irish souse who was so bow-legged he didn't *need* to go on a bender?

*　　*　　*

Did you hear about the sick old Irishman who married for money? He's a preacher.

*　　*　　*

Did you hear about the Irish golfer who keeps getting slung out of different clubs? He's resigned to it.

* * *

Did you hear about the Irish Toy manufacturer? His wife has to wind him up before he can perform.

* * *

Did you hear about the Irish movie mogul who turned down Raquel Welch for the lead in his new movie because she had flat feet?

* * *

Did you hear about the bankrupt Irishman who tried to gas himself in the oven but discovered that the Electricity Board had cut it off because the account was overdue?

* * *

Did you hear about the Irish millionaire who always takes a taxi when he sleep-walks?

* * *

Did you hear about the ambitious Irishman who only had one aim in life, and he missed?

* * *

Did you hear about the Irishman who couldn't find a Japanese sandman to repair his egg-timer? He became a poacher.

*   *   *

Did you hear about the very inebriated Irish couple? He was in his cups, *and* he was in her cups.

*   *   *

Did you hear about the stern Irish father who waits up for his daughter and searches her for fingerprints?

*   *   *

Did you hear about the Irish author who's written a *Who's Who* of leading African politicians and given the book the title 'Who Dat?'?

*   *   *

Did you hear about the Irish girl who's been spraying toilet water behind her ears? She doesn't know what she will do after the cistern has been repaired.

*   *   *

Did you hear about the Irishman who has been reading a very interesting kind of book that he found in his wife's jewel-box? It's a sort of 'whodunit'.

*   *   *

Did you hear about the Irishman who was a guest at a Royal Command Performance in Belfast? Prince Philip told him to belt up.

*   *   *

An Irishman was astonished when a coloured man on his bus collected his money and handed out the ticket all in a matter of a quarter of a second. He suspects it was a lightning conductor.

*   *   *

Did you hear about the Irish guy whose wife was flat-chested and big with it? She kept taking her chest into other guys' flats.

*   *   *

Did you hear about the Irishman who was so ugly and horrible that when Alfred Hitchcock passed him on the way to the graveyard he fainted? The Irishman, not Hitchcock.

*   *   *

'Have a pinch, Paddy?'
'No, tanks. I don't take snuff.'
'What do you mean, snuff? This is arsenic.'

*   *   *

Patrick has a very good war record. Vera Lynn singing 'There'll be green birds over the green cliffs of Dover . . .'

*   *   *

O'Hagen showed his neighbour a letter which had been anonymously delivered to his home. It stated: 'If you don't stop taking liberties with my wife, I am going to kill you.'

The neighbour said, 'Oh don't worry about that. Practically every man in the street has had the same warning.'

*   *   *

O'Grady went to the optician and asked if they sold monocles.

'Yes, we have just received a new consignment,' he was told.

'Good, den, now I can have one for each eye.'

*   *   *

An Irish cyclist went to the supply shop and asked for a pair of bicycle clips. The man said, 'Look, you are pedalling with only long stockings. You don't *need* cycle clips because you have short trousers.'

The racing champ said, 'I know dat, don't I, you idgit! But I got to have *something* to stop me hair falling over me face.'

*   *   *

'I'm having to go over to Phoenix Park to tell me old mother some news, who's riding in the Six Day Bicycle Race.'

'Don't be daft, the Six-Day Bicycle Race finished three days since.'

'That's what I have to tell me old Mam.'

*   *   *

Did you hear about the Irishman who had a Jumbo Jet crash into his council house because he left the landing light on?

*   *   *

Or the Irishman who gave pianola concerts all over the Bortsch Curcuit under the name of Paddy Russki?

*   *   *

Or the Irish labourer who claimed allowances for coming from a broken home while he was working as a demolition contractor?

*   *   *

Or the Irishman who used to shout at his pigeons to keep them on their pigeon toes and was fined for using fowl language?

*   *   *

Or the Irishman who had his trousers made without zips or buttons because there were no flies on him?

*   *   *

Or the Irishman who only paid half-rate on the railway because he wasn't all there?

*   *   *

Or the Irish barber who went to the doctor for some powders for the woodworm in his sideboards?

*   *   *

Or the Irishman who heard about the bitter cold outside, but couldn't find any because it was probably hidden in the snow?

*   *   *

Or the Irishman who wanted to get his trousers repaired and couldn't because all the menders were invisible?

*   *   *

Or the Irish pop star whose current release on the Green Label ran into four noughts – he sold none in Ireland, none in England, none in Scotland and none in Russia?

*   *   *

Or the Irishman who was so knock-kneed he had to play the cello side-saddle and his crotchet got pinched?

*   *   *

Or the Irish rustler who ran out of cellophane?

*   *   *

Or the Irish masseur who rubbed shoulders with the gentry?

* * *

Or the Irishman who had an accident on the morning tube? His toothbrush got stuck in it.

* * *

Or the Irish celebrity who had all his business cards whitewashed over because he wanted to be anonymous?

* * *

Or the Irish toastmaster who used to pop out of bed when he felt browned off?

* * *

What about the Irish karate champion who swatted a fly on his chin and broke his neck?

* * *

What about the Irishman who brought home a monkey, a parrot and a hare and told his wife they would have to sleep under the bed so as to keep warm. She said, 'But what about the smell?' And he replied, 'They'll just have to get used to it.'

* * *

What can you call an Irish-Jewish person who has never been circumcised? A Kosher Colleen.

*　　*　　*

Two Irish couples had a holiday coming up so they decided to experiment in a novel situation by exchanging partners to see if it improved married life. The day after the swop-over one of the husbands said, 'That was very agreeable, and I'm glad we thought of it.' The other man said, 'Me too, but let's go and see how the women are getting along.'

*　　*　　*

What about the Irish terrier who saw a sign stating 'Wet Paint' and immediately obeyed.

*　　*　　*

An Irish boy met and married a Jewish girl, and in the fullness of time they produced a little Lepracohen.

*　　*　　*

One Irishman said, 'What does a man who has five girlfriends do about breakfast?' The other one said, 'Oh I usually have some Energen bread, three bowls of oats and a pot of Rhinoceros-horn tea.'

*　　*　　*

An Irishman was arrested for decency because he ran through a Nudist's Lido fully clad.

*　　*　　*

The girl said to the Irishman, 'If you like, we can go to my room and make love.' He said, 'What a clever idea. You go ahead and if I'm not there in ten minutes, start without me.'

*　　*　　*

The police mistakenly raided the Irishman after a tip-off suggesting he hoarded pornographic material. Indignantly he complained, 'Bejabers, I don't *even have* a pornograph!'

*　　*　　*

Paddy said, 'How did the Queen know she was going to have a baby?' O'Malley said, 'Are you daft? It was announced in all the papers.'

*　　*　　*

Old Pat Regan was 78 years old and he suddenly announced that he was going to marry a 22-year-old girl. His eldest son said, 'You're crazy. You're long past it. I warn you – it could be fatal.' The old boy shrugged and said, 'If she dies, son, she dies.'

*　　*　　*

'What a lovely healthy cow you have there, Farmer Kelly. I loike de colour of him, so I do.'
'Yes, Finnigan. It's a very expensive Jersey.'
'Oh, pardon me den, I tought it was its skin.'

*　　*　　*

An Irishman was invited to be one of the speakers at a meeting concerning the growing promiscuity among the local population and its effect on church attendance. After six other speakers had had their say, the Irishman stood up to a volley of applause. Said he, 'Ladies and gentlemen, it gives me great pleasure.' Then he sat down.

*   *   *

'Do you have sex relations?' Riley asked his friend. 'Indeed I do,' said O'Malley. 'I have three cousins who are boys, three aunts who are women and an old grandfather over by Galway.'

*   *   *

Randy O'Toole passed by one of his workmates crossing the street and inquired casually, 'How is that lovely, cheerful, darlin' wife of yours, Finigan, and all our bonny kiddies?'

*   *   *

Said Riley, 'My wife is so blind, she can't even recognize her friends until they're on top of her.'

*   *   *

He scored two tries in the Rugger final at Twickenham He also scored twice at the Belfast Stadium, but that was after the match.

*   *   *

Short-sighted Dr O'Grady went on a shoot with friends and was tickled pink when he brought down something which he thought could well be a rare bird. 'What would be the species of fowl I have just winged?' he yelled to one of the beaters.

'Master,' the beater answered, 'between calling you a bald-headed, skunk-faced idiot he says his name's Murphy.'

* * *

The doctor delivered the child safely and said to Mrs Rafferty, 'Bejabers, the little whippersnapper only weighs a meagre nineteen ounces!' The husband butted in, 'Well what would you be expecting Dr Douglas, and me and Maureen only wed five weeks?'

* * *

They are going to call the new baby Hazel. Would you credit that! With all the saints and saintesses to choose from, they go and give the little lad the name of a nut!

* * *

A feller asked his girl's father for her hand in marriage. Pop asked, 'Well, the point is do you think you can make Corah happy?' He said, 'Heck, man, you ought to have seen her at the motel last night.'

* * *

Paddy claims French ancestry since his great-great grandfather was born in Lyons and was supposedly guillotined by Robespierre. Three or four times.

* * *

'Take me,' pleaded Dora. 'Take me, take me!'
Murphy said, 'No.'
'Please take me,' she insisted.
'No, no,' he said, 'I've already seen that stupid film *twice*.'

* * *

'Doctor, my husband keeps thinking he's a goods lift.'
'That's bad, you'd better bring him to see me.'
'Can't, Doctor, he doesn't stop at this floor!'

* * *

Patrick was working in the packing department of a firm renowned for its exquisite fragile pottery. He got worried one morning after a mishap and had to report to the boss. 'Sor,' said he, 'will you look at this now, your honour, sor – this foine piece of porcelain spoilt beyond redemption, such carelessness of the workmen, sor.'
The boss said, 'What workmen? The bloody dish was smashed by *you*!'
'Well not entirely, sor,' argued Pat. 'When I picked it up I noticed it was already a bit bent.'

* * *

The gang was arriving at the site. Paddy helped unload the trucks of tools and demolition gear, hampered by the intense cold and ice and raging, biting wind. Then he said, 'Never mind the elements. I'll soon have a foine big fire on the go,' and continued rubbing the two sticks of dynamite together.

* * *

When she was pregnant she had an enormous appetite. Once she was so starved I said, 'Would you like a Penguin? And she said, 'Blimey, you're sure right, but do you know how to shoot one?'

*   *   *

Ernie-boy is so brilliant that if he sees a notice reading 'This Lift Is Only Made To Take Seven Persons' he waits around until another six people show up.

*   *   *

Paddy sells good books, door to door. He even tried to sell a bible to the vicar at the local church, but the vicar refused because it was in a foreign language – the original Hebrew.

*   *   *

Did you hear about the Irishman whose colleen was not allowed to drink anything stronger than pop? She had no problem because her pop drank anything and everything, on or under the bar.

*   *   *

Did you hear about the Irish fruit and dairy farmer who sacked four of his milkmaids because they couldn't keep their calves together? *And* the head cowman was severely envied.

*   *   *

Did you hear about Shaun who underwent a medical for the Ulster Rifles and was even turned down for a citizen?

*　　*　　*

Did you hear about the absent-minded Irishman? He still can't remember where he left it.

*　　*　　*

Have you heard about the absent-minded Irishman who tied a knot in his pyjamas to remind himself where his bedroom was, and then ruptured himself trying to stuggle into the legs?

*　　*　　*

Did you hear about the Irish middle-weight champion of the district who was knocked out in the second round and had to be helped to the canvas?

*　　*　　*

Did you hear about the Irish-born Persian cat who never wees on the floor because he brought his own strip of carpet?

*　　*　　*

A suspect Irishman was waved down by the police on the main road. The sergeant asked if he could look inside the boot. The suspect took his shoes and socks off.

*　　*　　*

Because he prefers pet fish to pet dogs Shaun is training his goldfish to come to heel.

*   *   *

Have you heard about the disillusioned Irishman who went due South-East to join the North-West Foreign Legion and found himself commanding a Brownie group as Brown Owl O'Toole?

*   *   *

Did you hear about the old Irish tourist who was standing on the high cliffs above the sea when an enormous flight of migrant birds coursed across the skyline? A passing ornothologist noted the Irishman's disbelief and said, 'Where do you think all these wild geese have come from?' The Irishman considered for an hour, then shrugged and said, 'Eggs, I should tink.'

*   *   *

Did you hear about the unfortunate Irish pile-driver who was deafened by the noise and suffered severely from insomnia? The company doctor was another Irishman fortunately, and he advised him to rest more and to get more sleep.

*   *   *

Did you hear about the poor Irishman whose trousers were old, baggy and as shiny as a mirror? In fact, when he rent them and they split into pieces he had seven years bad luck.

*   *   *

Or the Irishman who entered an Irish bicycle in the six-day National Cycle Race and it fell apart after six hours?

* * *

Did you hear about the indolent Irish tinker who relinquished his profession as a cutler because he found the work too much of a grind?

* * *

Did you hear about the Irishman who finally got free of the seven-year-itch? He found the flea.

* * *

'What's good for a splitting headache?'
'Have you tried using a sharp axe?'

* * *

Have you heard about the Irish mystery man who wears a blank identity disk because he wants to stay anonymous?

* * *

He wanted to go into the army, but because he was only eight years old he could only enlist in the infantry.

* * *

Mike went into the café and ordered a dover sole and the waitress laid him a plaice.

*   *   *

Paddy was told by the Musical Director to get two saxophones from the BBC studio, and he returned with two bags full of GPO hand-set rejects.

*   *   *

Yesterday was a proper red-letter day. Paddy cut his lip opening an Income Tax demand note.

*   *   *

Catholic padres in Cork are so religious they eat nothing but anglers on Friday.

*   *   *

His wife wanted the new carpet laid quickly so she decided to lay it herself. They're the only family in the street with wall-to-wall latex underlay.

*   *   *

Paddy bought some rubber gloves so that he could wash his hands without getting his fingers wet.

*   *   *

The insurance money was so little, Paddy often wishes his mother-in-law hadn't fallen out of the window.

*   *   *

'And remember – the Neutron Bomb could open up a whole new world for you,' said the Irish lecturer.

*　　*　　*

Sean was very ill but he's recovering now. You can tell because he's back blowing the foam off his syrup of figs.

*　　*　　*

Patrick took his visitor to his local pub for a session and the visitor said it was quaint to see sawdust strewn on the floor in country fashion. He didn't know that it was the previous evening's furniture.

*　　*　　*

He's suffering from an in-going saloon door.

*　　*　　*

Murphy opened a restaurant in Belfast and his first customer from Texas commended him, 'Murphy, what a great Bolognese you served up!'
Murphy said, 'Sure, and the aim is we *got to feature* the local menus.'

*　　*　　*

Mrs O'Neil ruined a garment she was making and she shouted, 'Now what blathering sew-and-sew of a husband is it who's been mending his socks with me appliance!'

*　　*　　*

Mike's mate on the site was climbing a ladder with a hod full of bricks when he slipped and dropped the lot on top of his head. 'Hell's bells,' he laughed, 'it's hailing great slabs, and not a cloud in the sky.'

* * *

Cautious drinkers in Killkenny mistrust the local water supply so they fluoride it, filter it, boil it and then drink Guinness instead.

* * *

Battered Mike told the doctor, 'I keep thinking I'm a bridge. I don't know what's come over me.' And the doctor said, 'Five trucks, a bus and a squad car.'

* * *

Mick knows all about cars. He's won most of his formula races – his formula is two of brandy, one of scotch and a squirt of bitters. At the last international trials he notched up 33 pit stops. Two for burst tyres and 31 to ask the way.

* * *

To keep down the rising birthrate among animals, Belfast Zoo has shot all the storks.

* * *

McReady is so positive in his belief in reincarnation he's left all his money to himself, C.O.D.

* * *

A father of ten was accidentally shot yesterday while running across a field. Someone mistook him for a rabbit.

*   *   *

The local newspaper has recently printed information garnered from Irish industrial reporters. Here are some samples:
Our men have been on strike so often, this year the works outing is going to be an organized visit round the factory.

*   *   *

It pays to join our union. If the foreman gives you a job to do, we fight the case for you.

*   *   *

The Irish Government warns that birth control is useless unless it's put into practice nine months before the actual birth.

*   *   *

The Irish judge released a man from custody and dismissed all the police accusations against him for gross indecency. It seems that on a recount the villain had only done it 143 times.

*   *   *

The Irish goal-keeper was very distressed as the team ran into the dressing room. He was the only one in the entire club that nobody kissed.

* * *

He bought two acres of building land yesterday. At midnight he was still loading it on his lorry.

* * *

I shared a room with him once. I said, 'O'Mally, you should put on a clean pair of socks every day.' He did what I said every morning. After a week he couldn't get his boots on.

* * *

My neighbour is so stupid. If you say 'good morning' to him he's stuck for an answer.

* * *

Pat told me that he was late because of Divine Service. I thought he meant he'd been to church, but I found out it was a local massage parlour.

* * *

Our typist's stupid. She answers the phone every time her typewriter bell rings.

* * *

Pat's little boy is only six and he does bird impressions. He eats worms.

* * *

Irish lifts are so slow, they show movies between floors.

* * *

You know the kind of town that it is – every Tom, Dick and Harry is called Paddy.

* * *

BIG MURPHY
- once tried to get a two-way bet on the Boat Race.
- is more than a drop-out – his navel contemplates *him*.
- only breeds St Bernard dogs for the brandy.
- has hair so long when he has a beer-shampoo he gets a hangover for the next three days.
- steals cars. They banned him from driving last week. Now he only steals chauffeur-driven cars.

* * *

Murphy's wife's so fond of her dog, when it rains she sends her husband out to bark at strangers.

* * *

Murphy said: 'Our dog's just eaten all the clocks in the house. Surprising really – it's meant to be a watch dog.'

* * *

The building labourer asked the boss, 'What's a cubic foot?'
'I don't know,' said the boss, 'ask your shop-steward, he pretends to know everything.'
So the labourer said, 'Shop-steward, what's a cubic foot?'
The shop-steward said, 'I don't know, son, but you find out and I'll get you compensation for it.'

* * *

Not many people know that an Irishman named O'Connor invented the loo seat in 1866. In 1868 it was improved upon when a Scot named MacTollugh cut a hole in the middle.

* * *

This Irish character is at the bar muttering to himself nastily because he's just paid for thirteen pints of beer and he's trying to find a way to transport them across the ale-house to his mates. The bar owner says to him, 'Would you like a tray?'
Says the Irishman belligerently, 'Are you trying to be funny? I've got *enough* to carry as it is!'

* * *

'And when I die,' said Murphy to Andrew, 'I am going to leave you all the money dat you owe me.'

* * *

From the *Cork Courier*:
'The recession's affecting everyone. Next year the Queen's going to have the Trooping of the Colour in black and white.'

*   *   *

An Irish saleslady was arrested last night. She was demonstrating the strength of the elastic in a new lycra brassière when her knickers fell down.

*   *   *

What do you get when you tip scalding water down a rabbit-hole? You get hot, cross bunnies, says Paddy.

*   *   *

Muggins put a notice in the local newspaper worded: 'Will the thief who nicked my ladder from my back yard return it immediately or further steps will be taken.'

*   *   *

Paddy is terribly intelligent. He repeats everything the parrot says.

*   *   *

Fiona went out three nights running with the Bionic man and was taken to hospital with metal fatigue.

*   *   *

Clancy is a bar-room artist. He sits there most of the time drawing corks.

*   *   *

The police asked the girl, 'This man you say raped you four times in the park . . . do you mean that you cannot give us *any* description at all? His height, colour, weight – nothing?' The girl shrugged, 'No. Nothing.' The detective said, 'That's got us beat.'
The girl said, 'Well I'm sorry, sergeant, but I *always* shut my eyes when I'm being kissed.'

*　　*　　*

The crook waylaid Peg in the dark and threatened her: 'All right lady, this is a stick-up.' And she said, 'Thank heavens – for a minute I thought you were a mugger!'

*　　*　　*

One of the girls working at the hotel complained to the manager that she had been raped. The manager said, 'Well, I've always warned you to watch out for forged Travellers' Cheques.'

*　　*　　*

So this girl went to the railway office and demanded to see the top official stationmaster, and she said, 'All the way to Boggan one of your damned porters kept sneaking into my sleeping compartment!'
The stationmaster said, 'Good God, woman, what do you expect on a cheap Awayday ticket – the Minister of Transport?'

*　　*　　*

35

Maureen went into the tobacconist's shop and asked to see some 19½-inch cigarette-holders . . . She hates the ash trickling down her bodice.

*   *   *

Murphy bought a car on the instalment plan because of inflated prices. So far he's bought two wheels and a wing-mirror – and next week, a door . . .

*   *   *

The Mulligan family went abroad this year for their annual hols. They toured the continent so fast they did the whole of Rome in eighty minutes. In fact they were in and out of the Vatican so quickly, God said, 'Who in hell was that?'

*   *   *

Paddy was marooned on a desert island until one afternoon the tide washed ashore a large rowing-boat. Paddy broke it up and built himself a raft.

*   *   *

Semus had been sitting close to the confession box for a long time before Father O'Malley spotted him.
'Boy! Just how long have you been waiting there? Have you been listening to confessions all evening?'
'Cripes, no, Father O'Malley,' stuttered the lad, 'I'm only here since that woman who slept with all those sailors came out laughing.'

*   *   *

Clancey was singing noisily and out of tune as he milked the cow in the barn. When the farmer heard the racket he went to the cowshed and got the pitchfork and shouted to Clancey, 'Will you shut the racket, you noisy poltroon!' Clancey shouted back, 'I'm only trying to calm her down. Did you ever try milking a cow that's all of a tremble?' The farmer said, 'You idiot, it's *your* noise that's shuddering her udders.' Clancey shouted back, 'Well I don't have no such trouble with your daughter Maggie.'

* * *

An Irish girl who had played the field went in search of one of her friends and asked a neighbour where he might be at. 'Since he's the man who plays the organ a lot, no doubt you'll be finding him down at the music school orchestrating the choir.'
Said the colleen, 'The spalpeen! He's spiting me by eliminating the competition!'

* * *

Every night Shamus used to make love over the telephone, but the council put an end to it yesterday – they evicted the couple because they wanted to repaint the kiosk.

* * *

One of the two gay Irish poets went into the little church because he wanted to light a candle to the virgin fairy.

* * *

Murphy knocked the stuffing out of Pat because he interfered with his clothing – he sent it to the Chinese laundry instead of the Washeteria.

* * *

Then there's the Irish optician who made Father O'Malley a new set of spectacles with stained-glass lenses.

* * *

Then there's the Irish politician who insisted that he could introduce a five-year-plan for rehousing the homeless community, and do it in three years.

* * *

An Irish snob is a man who goes to the opera with a copy of the script, a packing of chewing gum and two sleeping pills.

* * *

The Irishman visited his priest for information and asked if it was all right to have intercourse before marriage and the priest said, 'No, my son – you might block the aisle.'

* * *

The Catholic priest with the ramshackle motor finally capitulated and sold the vehicle. Frankly he didn't have the vocabulary to keep it on the road.

* * *

An Irish beauty who was endowed with a magnificent singing voice as well as a voluptuous figure discussed a contract to sing in an Irish Club. The agent said, 'I'll pay you £50 a session, six nights and one matinee.' The singer asked, 'Is that for each, or both?'

*　　*　　*

Then there was the Irish hypochondriac who kept well away from the red-light area of Ballymoony because he couldn't tolerate hormones.

*　　*　　*

One Irishman phoned another and said, 'Come on over, we're having a wake.'
His friend said, 'I dunno, we've got a bad case of insipient laryngitis in the house.' 'What the hell,' said the other Irishman, 'this lot here will drink *anything*; just bring it.'

*　　*　　*

Three Irishmen were arrested on the border for smuggling pigs out of the Republic into Northern Ireland. As they were being taken to the nick one said, 'We've been double-crossed. Someone squealed on us.'
Another said, 'You're right. It must have been the *sow* shopped us!'

*　　*　　*

Only an Irishman can be in two different places at the same time and talking about it from somewhere else.

*　　*　　*

41

Shaun the poster-man was doing a sign for the Irish Dance Hall last week and it read. '*All* Ladies and Gentlemen Are Welcome – Regardless of Sex.'

*   *   *

I met an Irish visitor on the platform and he was crying his eyes out. I asked him if he was already homesick, and he cried, 'No. I've lost all me luggage!' So I asked how that happened and he said, 'The cork fell out.'

*   *   *

The Irish Premier has had to notify the press that he has abandoned the attempt to put a man on the moon. They can't find a Guinness bottle big enough to hold the stick the astronaut is screwed to.

*   *   *

Mike complained to the Chinese manager of the take-away, 'There's a small cockroach in me bird's-nest soup.' And he said, 'Ah so! You wait two minutes, we find you big one.'

*   *   *

Shaun ordered a Welsh Rabbit and when the waiter brought it, it was still singing.

*   *   *

Shaun spent three hours digging into eight feet of snow to clear his drive so that he could motor to work. Then he remembered he didn't have a car.

*   *   *

The chippie told his mate, 'My old man had steel nerves. In the last war he flew Wellingtons, single-handed – and to prove it, I'm still wearing 'em.'

*   *   *

Jack O'Hagen sleeps rough, all around the country. He's Jack the Kipper.

*   *   *

Farmer O'Hara of Ballymena died yesterday from too much milk. One of his cows fell on him.

*   *   *

Patrick thinks that the Gaza Strip is a Jewish night-club cabaret feature.

*   *   *

Teacher asked little Patrick how he would divide sixteen Irish potatoes equally between seventeen people. Pat said he'd serve Wondermash.

*   *   *

Sean had to have a medical before starting his new job as a brick-tester. Three psychiatrists examined his brain for an hour but didn't find anything.

* * *

At school little Pat was asked by the teacher how Noah managed to gather the animals into the ark after dark and he said, 'No problem. He had a lot of Isra-lights.'

* * *

There's a very wealthy family of Irish farmers near Kilkenny. Every Friday the family has a party with Rolls Cornish Pasties . . . and Leprecorn liquor.

* * *

When O'Hara learned about the Arab oil crisis he said, 'Begorra, dem wogs has got us over a barrel.'

* * *

Then there's the Irish traffic cop who couldn't cope with a broken-down Hartley's lorry because of the big jam.

* * *

O'Hagen got a job as a crossing warden, but he wouldn't let anyone go over the road unless they were a zebra.

* * *

Mulligan went home and made himself a cocktail – a pint of Guinness, an egg-cupful of Irish Whisky and a peeled potato, dropped down the side.

* * *

Fiona found her husband Murphy wearing a clean shirt that was saturated. 'What did you do that for, ye cretin!' Murph said, 'Well, I read the label and it said "wash and wear"!'

* * *

A policeman met Mike and noticed he was walking with an enormous ten-ton elephant, so he asked him where he got it. Mike said he found it. The policeman said, 'Then take it to the zoo.'
At suppertime the policeman met Mike again, and he said sharply, 'I thought I told you to take that beast to the local zoo!'
Mike said, 'I did, I did, and he says he wants to go *again* tomorrow.'

* * *

Paddy wanted to tell the kids a smashing bedside story, but he couldn't because it hadn't been made up yet.

* * *

Pat bought a hot dog to guard the family valuables and it slept on the stove because it was a range rover.

* * *

Paddy went to bed with his wife and a tape measure. because he wanted to know how long she'd be.

* * *

O'Hagan's wife was invited to a fancy dress ball and she went as a Partridge to show how game she was.

* * *

In an Irish restaurant, having dinner, I asked the waiter if he would bring us another candle, and he said, 'Yes, sor. With or without cream?'

* * *

Once upon a time there was an Irish red-Indian who flashed a message thirty miles using smoke signals. The message read: 'Help! I have set my blanket on fire.'

* * *

A Britannica salesman knocked on Casey's door and wasted three hours trying to sell him an encyclopedia for his lad, Pete. Said Casey, 'Let the lad walk to school, the way I had to.'

* * *

Dim Dora hired a firm of private detectives to find out if the baby was really hers.

* * *

Clodagh and Pat have just ended a life-long friendship. They got married.

*　　*　　*

Pat had this Bullworker for six months and still can't open a sauce bottle.

*　　*　　*

When Casey feels deaf, he knows it's time to go and get a haircut.

*　　*　　*

Pat's sister's got green fingers. Not for gardening – it's that engagement ring her boy bought her.

*　　*　　*

The Bishop was annoyed and told the vicar, 'Why did you fill Lord Marner's head with all that stuff about reincarnation?'
'Well,' said the vicar, ' he's ninety years old, so I thought a little talk about resurrection and reincarnation would cheer him up.'
The Bishop said, 'You dolt, he was going to leave us £300,000 in his will, and now he's gone and left it to himself.'

*　　*　　*

Then there's the Mother Inferior who has a wooden leg and who is known throughout the length and breadth of her body as Hop-a-long Chastity.

*　　*　　*

MOTHER IN LAW M'CREE

When they heard that she was going to Dublin for her holiday they declared it a disaster area.

* * *

The husband said, 'Oh I do wish I could do bird impressions,' and his wife asked why. He said, 'Well for one thing, I wouldn't half spoil your mother's new hat.'

* * *

I'm not saying she's old, although it's a fact she was at the Boston Tea Party some years back. She was the first bag they threw overboard.

* * *

I know what I'll get her for her birthday . . . a G-Plan dining trough.

* * *

When she went down to the Citizens' Advice Bureau, they advised her to get out of town.

* * *

You can tell how lonely she was, when she went to the Over-Fifty Club, she took a chap from Rent-a-Bloke.

* * *

She was so cold in bed one night the following morning she went to the electricity office, bought eighty yards of pink flex and knitted herself a blanket.

*   *   *

She played in 'Fairy Tales' . . . the glass slipper fitted her perfectly, but when she kissed the handsome prince, he turned into a toad.

*   *   *

A low neckline suits her a treat: it goes with her character and upbringing.

*   *   *

McManus knocks on the door of a house and a woman comes to the door so he says, 'Could you lend a helping hand to a poor chap whose wife is out of work?'

*   *   *

He was so desperately tired that he was forced to knock up a chorus girl just to get a bed for the night.

*   *   *

Ireland imported four hundred tons of raw material from abroad last year, it says in my paper. That's three hundred tons of pornographic books from New York and a hundred tons of French postcards.

*   *   *

The first monk said to the second monk, 'Slattery, why are the chapel bells ringing this morning?' And the reply was, 'Because Brother Francis is pulling the perishing rope, you fool.'

*　　*　　*

There's a doughnut manufacturer in Tadgh who has never been so busy since last Easter. He's so behind with orders that he's had to subcontract the hole-making to another firm.

*　　*　　*

Shaun thinks it was John Gay who wrote 'The Begorrahs' Opera'.

*　　*　　*

An Irish woman was cuckolding her husband. One night the husband returned unexpectedly and caught her in a compromising position with his best friend Mr Lessing. He shrieked, 'How dare you entertain Mr Lessing while I'm away! I'll kill the swine. I'll murder the old buzzard.' He really was very angry. The wife pleaded, 'Don't kill him, Stanley. Be reasonable. Where do you think our apartment came from? And the Rolls-Royce? And the yacht? And my sable coat . . .' The husband paused and said, 'The car? The flat? Your pretty clothes? Not – not the colour TV, too?' His wife nodded miserably. The husband shrugged, put his gun away and said to his wife, 'Dora, don't let him stand around there with nothing on – get him my dressing-robe. He'll freeze to death!'

*　　*　　*

The Irish politician began his speech: 'There is something I want to get off my chest today that has been hanging over my head for weeks, and I'll be glad to put it behind me before we come to the end.'

*   *   *

Tough about the man who bought a book about how to make things disappear and someone pinched it.

*   *   *

Then there's the Irish magician who did tricks with a hare. When show-business dropped off, he got his assistant a job at the dog track.

*   *   *

Then there's the Irish illusionist who used to saw a woman in half on stage. One night he got more drunk than usual and did it sideways, and his assistant was so amused she fell about.

*   *   *

An unemployed Irishman was asked at the Jobcentre supermarket what he did for a living and he said he was a magician who did sleight of hand, so the Irish assistant sent him on to a building site to tile a roof.

*   *   *

Then there was that Irishman who bragged that he could go anywhere blindfolded, so a disbeliever challenged him to cross the River Guinness, and while he was scratching his back a passing firing squad shot him.

*   *   *

Then there's the luckless Irish tailor who sneaked into a secret wife-swapping orgy and got his own back.

*   *   *

He insisted that as a child he was a bottle-fed infant: he *could* have been breast-fed, but he *preferred* the Guinness.

*   *   *

When he landed, he went straight to the station and arrived in London at 2.30, stopped at an Irish hotel for a Guinness and then called at Moss Bros for a handout. He thought Moss was the Ministry of Social Security.

*   *   *

This Irishman started work on a farm and was a complete novice; when the farmer told him at lunchtime to make a milk shake, he got a stick and tried to make a cow jump up and down.

*   *   *

The national fruit of Ireland? Monkey-wrench nuts.

*   *   *

A man who owned an Irish Wolfhound thought he had gone a bit mad and needed some treatment, but when they got to the canine psychiatrist's consulting room, he wasn't allowed on the couch.

*   *   *

Then there's the Irish financier who can't kiss his wife at night because she had her teeth gold capped and sleeps with her head in the safe. He wouldn't have minded so much, but they were a matched set of dentures.

*   *   *

The doctor gave Pat a bottle of pills to improve his loss of memory, but he forgot where he hid them.

*   *   *

Then there's the urgent husband Murphy whose girl didn't believe in sex before marriage, and one night she caught him at it.

*   *   *

Did you hear about the poor little colleen who went to the hospital for shock treatment? One of the orderlies chased her around the consulting room with a vibrator.

*   *   *

Did you hear about Big Mike who wanted to send a stone of cauliflowers from Munich to Dublin, and retained Interflora?

* * *

Did you hear about the Irishman who was arrested for wearing a garment with two breast pockets? It was a brassière.

* * *

Did you hear about the Irishman who had his operation at a posh hotel in Ireland – it was a Truss House Forte?

* * *

Then there's Clancy who's wife told him: 'Remember to put the cat out,' and he couldn't, because he couldn't find the extinguisher.

* * *

Mike was sent to a government training centre and provided with an address where the landlady was a bit short on cooking expertise: three times a day through the first week of his ordeal he was served hare stew. Friday evening he was very sick. The landlady said, 'Perhaps I ought to send for the doctor, Michael?' Mike said in agony, 'Better still, Mrs Harris, send for a ferret.'

* * *

IS IT IRISH? An Irish Jew emigrated to the States and while he was in New York his son was born and he wished to have him circumcised. Being a stranger, he asked a cab driver where to find the Jewish circumciser and was directed to an address on 44th Street. The immigrant walked there, found a long street of shops and houses, and started looking for Number 4522. After hours of searching he failed to find the right address, so he stopped a policeman and told him he wanted the Jewish circumciser.

The cop said, 'Shure, it's the second doorway from where we're standing right this minute.'

The Jew went back along the street and saw that Number 4522 was a shop filled with a window of clocks – grandfather clocks, alarm clocks, cuckoo clocks, big clocks, wee clocks – hundreds of them crammed there. Then he realized that there was a door alongside the shop leading to a staircase going to the floor above, so he went up, and sure enough the circumciser Mr Feinbaum was up there. He made the arrangements and then said to Feinbaum, 'But tell me, why do you mislead people by filling the shop window with *clocks*?' The rabbi shrugged and said inquiringly, 'So vhat *vould* you expecting me put in mine vindow, Mr O'Isaacs?'

* * *

On Irish TV the other night the TV Cook said: 'And so you will find this very appetizing chicken dinner sufficient for four, and furthermore you can make a very nourishing broth from the remains if you have an invalid in the house.'

* * *

After he had made romantic love to her, the Cork schoolteacher started to cry, 'I don't know how I can face my class again, knowing that I have sinned twice.' He frowned and said, 'Twice?' She said, 'You're not leaving already, are you?'

* * *

The Labour member of the council was protesting about the Planning Committee's intention to build a gentlemen's convenience opposite the Town Hall. He shouted, 'If the local inhabitants of Colm stand for this they will stand for anything!'

* * *

Caroline is a nice girl who advertises in Cork showcases that she is prepared to model for nude artists.

* * *

George is making good in his new business which specializes in designing and making high fashions for very fat women. Previously he was an upholsterer.

* * *

Outside an old church in Dublin there is an enormous sign which reads: 'Enter Here All Ye Faithful And Find Heaven.' Going closer one finds a smaller type-written message reading: 'This door is kept locked on account of the draught.'

* * *

One of the typists, Dora, made a mistake in the office today and the boss made her stay over and do it all again.

* * *

The bishop was invited to dinner by a wealthy property shark in Dublin whose apartment was a spacious penthouse with art treasures all over the walls – pinups cut from *Playboy*. Mine host said to the bishop, 'Now how about a good stiff whisky for a start, my lord bishop?' 'Dear me,' said the cleric. 'I'd sooner commit adultery than imbibe strong liquor.' Said mine host, 'Who the hell wouldn't!!'

* * *

A rabbi and a Catholic priest were neighbours. They irked one another. The priest bought a Bentley; the rabbi went out and bought a Rolls Phantom. The priest had a new driveway built; the rabbi had his house remodelled. The priest was out early one morning, pouring water over his Bentley's bonnet. The rabbi called down to him, 'What a stupid way to fill the radiator.' The priest said, 'I'm not topping the radiator, I'm christening the car with holy water. And *you* can't do *that*.'
An hour later the priest was on his way to service when he saw the rabbi lying down under the rear of the Rolls-Royce with a hacksaw and a file in his hand, sawing off the end inch of the exhaust pipe.

* * *

Paddy received his account from his analyst for professional services. He sent the bill back with half the money and reminded the shrink that he had a split personality.

*   *   *

Ulster horticulturalists have gone on strike again. They are demanding shorter flowers and double the honey.

*   *   *

The trouble with Irish hotel staffs is that when they go on a go-slow strike, nobody notices the difference.

*   *   *

An announcement came over the loud-howler at the vast new Irish supermarket: 'Will the lady who lost the Irish Wolfhound please come to the meat department as quickly as possible.'

*   *   *

Paddy never runs around with married women. He always leaves his wife at home.

*   *   *

An Irish television programme has a new slant on quizzes. The producer asks guests pertinent questions and they have to guess which stupid idiot sent them in.

*   *   *

A businessman in Cork had the misfortune to lose the combination of his big office safe, so he rang up a friend in the Police Department and asked him to send over an expert safe-breaker from the prison to try and open the thing. Maloney was released temporarily to perform the operation, and the grateful industrialist asked the prisoner, 'What's the damage?' Maloney said, 'The last time I opened a safe I got £3,006.'

* * *

Paddy's wife said to him, 'Can you let me have two pounds? I've decided to give you cash for your birthday.'

* * *

The anxious father-to-be asked the pretty Irish nurse in the maternity block, 'It isn't another girl is it?' The nurse said, 'Well, the third from the right is.'

* * *

The warden at the prison silently led the unrepentent O'Raffety to the electric chair. 'Does you have a last request, boy?' asked the kindly warden. 'Yes,' said O'Raffety, 'would you hold me hand when they pull the lever?'

* * *

An Irish farmer crossed a Holsteiner bull with a Jersey cow and now he's got an animal that says, 'Noo?' instead of 'Moo!'

* * *

The Irish contender for the Golden Gloves went to the photographer and said, 'I want to have some full-length photographs took.
The Scottish photographer said, 'Certainly, sir.
When's your next fight with Sandy McMulley?'

*　　*　　*

Jamey O'Hagen was carrying a torch for Fiona McManas; he wanted to see her before he spent money on a blind date.

*　　*　　*

Paddy told his wife in the supermarket: 'Never mind the large, monster, family, economy size, woman, get the small expensive packet we can afford.'

*　　*　　*

Maureen is not a girl to squander her time. When the bathroom flooded after a burst, she taught the three bairns to swim while she waited for the plumber.

*　　*　　*

Sign in the window of an Optician's premises in Donegal: 'If you don't see what you want, you've come to the right place.'

*　　*　　*

O'Malley says that poverty stares him in the face. His wife has given him sinus trouble – she's always nattering, 'Sinus a cheque for this; sinus a cheque for dat.'

* * *

Fiona, plaintively: 'Look, there's a ladder in these stockings!'
Cafferkey: 'What do you want, a marble staircase?'

* * *

Shaun said, 'That woman doesn't know how harsh words can hurt a body.'
'What did she say,' asked Keith.
'She said nothing – she threw the Britannica dictionary at me head.'

* * *

O'Neil was watching an angler catch two enormous carp with successive casts, then throw them back in the water. Ten minutes later he caught a cheeky little perch, which he landed and bagged. O'Neill asked the fisherman why he had discarded the two magnificent carp. 'It's like this,' said the angler, 'I only have a very small fry-pan.'

* * *

Mooney really felt that he needed a lot more exercise and he had to lie down for a whole hour before the urge wore off.

* * *

Many years back, when the countryside had poor lighting facilities, a farmer was helping with the birth of his newest addition by holding out a very ancient ornate oil-burning lamp invented by his grandfather, O'Toole. When three new offspring had been safely delivered by the rural Doc, the farmer panicked and bolted from the bedroom because the Doc indicated two more were on the way. 'Come back here with that perishing light,' roared the doctor.

The anguished father snorted, 'I will not, that I won't. It's the damned light that's attracting 'em.'

* * *

Two Irish explorers were lost in a snowy mountain range and at the point of exhaustion when they espied a bulky image materializing through the gloom. Mike's keen eye spied the St Bernard first and he observed that local monks must have sent a search party behind the animal. There, swinging from the St Bernard's collar, was the traditional little barrel of Irish brandy. 'Here comes man's best friend, bejabers!' cried Mike with relief. 'Yes,' said Kelly, 'and just look at that enormous old dog with it.'

* * *

A new doctor in County Wexford had to keep reminding his secretary to tell patients that he had a slight attack of laryngitis and NOT that he was a horse doctor.

* * *

Murphy applied to his boss for an increase in wages and the application was turned down. Murphy refused to be fobbed off and suggested, 'Well, if you can't manage an increase, how about you give me the same wages, but oftener?'

*   *   *

Casey wasn't having much luck courting his beloved and he said, 'Kathleen, you won't like it a bit if I shoot myself in me misery.' She said, 'Indeed I won't – I hate the sight of blood.'

*   *   *

There were two elderly hermits who owned small private islands just off the Irish coast. They only very rarely met, but one day they accidentally met while out in their little rowboats and they talked for three minutes about the state of the world. Another ten years passed before the older neighbour rowed over to the other's island and knocked on the cabin. 'Hello. Forget something?' asked his neighbour.

*   *   *

The Irish referee at the big fight had to interfere when Flanagan's trainer told his man, 'Look, will ye stop knocking the champ down, you fool, he's getting too much rest.'

*   *   *

They were watching the deep end of the pool, where a contest was in progress for the longest underwater dive. O'Malley said to the diver's coach, 'Does ye realize that if your boy comes up, this could be the international record for staying down under water!'

*　　*　　*

One Irish glowworm said to the other, 'Heck, have you only just shown up? I must have been chatting to this cigarette-end for hours.'

*　　*　　*

An Irish Television enthusiast was talking about all the violence in some programmes. 'They don't give you a chance,' he said. 'I was switching from the western over to the Church Service, and as I reached for the dial, I almost got my hand shot off!'

*　　*　　*

The diner said, 'Waiter, this steak is not the least bit tender.' The waiter, Clancy O'Toole, said in a soft brogue, 'Well, sor, it's like this, if it's love and affection yez wantin', why not try the little colleen at the pay-desk?'

*　　*　　*

O'Regan has found the way to make ends meet – he burns the candle at both ends.

*　　*　　*

O'Connor licked the hooch bug and was highly recommended by Alcoholics Unanimous. He says he wants to write his life story, but he can't remember more than a few days.

* * *

Says O'Hara: 'The best way to have money jingling in your pocket is to shake a leg there.'

* * *

The judge asked Kelly, 'Have you, at any time, in this court or any other court appeared as a witness?'
Kelly said, 'Yes, your honour.'
'In which suit were you acting as such a witness?' asked the judge.
'Me single-breasted, navy-striped reefer and drainpipe trousers, your honour. All good Irish tweed.'

* * *

Kelly's wife said, 'We'll have to go out for a meal. I couldn't make anything 'cos of the electric cut.'
Kelly said, 'We don't cook wid electrics, woman. We're all gas.'
She said, 'So are you – have you forgot we have an electric can-opener?'

* * *

O'Shauhnessy is confused; if matches are made in heaven, he wants to know where cigarette lighters came from.

* * *

'O'Hagan, how is it that you gave that carpark attendant a £1 tip?' O'Hagan said, 'Why not. Look at the almost new Jaguar *he* gave me.'

*　　*　　*

The well-known popular crook Peter O'Tarbeck is lying low. The bed sags badly in the middle.

*　　*　　*

Outside a jewellery store in Castelbar there's a sign advertising: 'Ears pierced while you wait, £3. Or instalments £4.'

*　　*　　*

In the *Irish Courier*: Ad. – 'Urgent aid needed. Belfast. Fourth baby in three weeks. Time off.'

*　　*　　*

Road sign noted in Cork:
'When this sign is under water the road is closed for traffic.'

*　　*　　*

On holiday O'Grady and wife went to a café and she said to the waitress, 'We want a pot of tea, and buns, and lots of hot water.' O'Grady went ashen, leaned across and said to his wife, 'You're not havin' a baby in here are yeh?'

*　　*　　*

An Irish farmer was selling some stock and the buyer asked how many animals were in the field. 'I don't know,' said the farmer. 'I'll have to count them.' Then he looked over the field and eventually said, 'Three hundred and twenty two.' The buyer asked, 'How did you count so fast?'

'Easy,' said the farmer. 'I just counted all the legs and divided by four.'

*   *   *

'This match won't light,' said the Irishman's wife.
'That's odd,' said her husband, 'it lit last night.'

*   *   *

Irish farmer in chemist's shop: 'I want three bars of that white soap.'
Chemist: 'Scented?'
Farmer: 'No, I'll take it with me.'

*   *   *

'Why did you walk into my shop backwards?'
'I figured you'd pay more attention if I was going out.'

*   *   *

A visitor to London from Wexford was intrigued by the music stool he saw in a city store, so he bought it. Eight years later he was in the area again on business, so he dropped in and button-holed the manager. 'That music stool you sold me years ago still hasn't uttered a note of music,' he said, 'but I'll be patient.'

*   *   *

Shaun saw Brendon struggling up the steep cobbled street with an enormous solid mahogany dining-table on his back. 'Is it some manner of a bet, you rupture yeself that way?' asked Shaun. 'Of course not,' scoffed Brendon, 'I'm taking it to the drapery store to be matched for a cloth cover.'

*　　*　　*

'Is it the golf you're taking up now, Kelly?' asked his friend watching him on the course. 'Indaid it is,' acknowledged the beginner. 'Fifty-seven strokes it took!' His friend: 'That's good going for a new player.' 'Yes, indeed,' agreed the tyro, 'and next week-end I'm going to play the second hole.'

*　　*　　*

An Irish musician visiting his parent's village went into a general store and asked the young colleen if she could sell him an 'E' string. The girl blushed and said, 'I couldn't tell the he's from the she's, so would you go behind the curtain and select what you need!'

*　　*　　*

The Irish greengrocer had a phone order from a local lady asking to send round a dozen peaches. He duly filled the order, but the lady rang again shortly after and complained that the man had only sent eleven peaches.
'I know,' he acknowledged, 'but one of them was rotted, so I threw it away for you.'

*　　*　　*

An Irishman gave his friend a birthday present of a grubby old book called 'How To Become A Millionaire'. His friend wasn't pleased because half the pages were torn away.

Said the donor, 'Well you won't turn up your nose at half a million, will you?'

*　　*　　*

A nervous crook, new to the game, anxiously walked into a pawnbroker's premises owned by a canny Irishman named Flannery. He stammered, 'Hands up or I'll shoot!' Flannery said, 'I'll give you £15 for the gun.'

'Done,' said the crook.

*　　*　　*

Fresh out of Ballyclonen, an Irish youth inquired at the railroad station, 'How do I get the train to Liverpool.'

The station attendant snapped, 'Get across the bridge quickly, the train goes to Liverpool in five minutes.'

The youth said, 'That's incredible progress! It took me longer than that on the bus to the station!'

*　　*　　*

Lanigan advertised in the 'Irish Times' for pen pals and got favourable replies from a styful of pigs.

*　　*　　*

The grocer complained to Brady that with every dozen eggs he supplied there were three or four pale shells containing nothing. The supplier said, 'That's odd. Leave it to me and I'll get the vet to check up.' So he got hold of Kinkelly the vet and they went to the farm. The vet glared at the Rhode Island with disapproval, then went into the hen house and snapped, 'All right, yous artful layabouts who *ain't* laying about . . . which of yez is on the pill?'

* * *

Cheerful Father O'Malley stopped Sean on his way into church and asked him, 'Look Sean, could you come back tomorrow night for confession? We have literally dozens and dozens in the church right now, and I'm sure that *you* haven't been stealing the crown jewels lately.'
'Of course I haven't, Father,' Sean smiled. On his way out he bumped into his pal, Liam, and caught him by the shoulder.
'Hold it, fat-face. Go home and come back tomorrow, because they're only hearing thieves and swindlers tonight.'

* * *

This Irish hold-up man dashed into Barclays Bank in Connymally and hissed, 'Listen, you, this is a cock-up,' and pushed two fingers through the grill.
The terrified clerk stammered, 'You mean it's *a stick up*!'
'No,' said the thief, 'I forgot to bring the gun!'

* * *

Visiting Ireland one summer, a tourist asked a local yokel the time. ' 'Tis twelve o'clock, your honour.' The stranger said, 'Surely it's later than that? Only twelve!' The yokel told him, 'It never gets later than that in these parts. After every twelve, it goes back to one.'

*　　*　　*

Cassidy confided in his best friend that he kept all his money at home hidden in a copper urn. The friend said, 'What's a copper urn?' And the other man said, 'Around £80 a week.' So his friend said, 'Don't you realize you're losing interest on your capital?' And the other genius said, 'No I'm not. I put away a little extra each week to cover the interest.'

*　　*　　*

An Irish astronaut had to go to London and the Government booked him into a 200-room, 100-storey hotel. He told the desk-clerk, 'Make it a basement suite. I can't stand heights.'
The clerk said, 'But you have to go millions of miles into the sky. How do you manage?'
'I just put my hands over my eyes and hope for the best.'

*　　*　　*

There is a road sign on the old boundary between Cullenen and Bradach which reads:
Bradach welcomes careful motorists. Every half hour a man is knocked down in Bradach. And he is getting sick and tired of it.

*　　*　　*

County Carey is noted for both its intense sexuality and its magnificent music. One young girl who lacked a husband, but was carrying a torch for one of her more productive partners thus hied herself to Belfast to consult a doctor. Searching the phone directory, she made the mistake of noting the number of a Doctor of Music, and called to make an appointment. The music doctor's daily maid took the call and told the anxious lass, 'Dr Carey can't come to the phone for the moment as he's over with the vicar, orchestrating *The Boys of Wexford*.'

'Oh!' stuttered the girl, 'I'm happy to hear it, but *tell him it's three months too late for me.*'

* * *

The tough owner of a private Irish bank hired an Irish detective to watch over things. He told the detective, 'I've no time for people trying to do me down. I prefer men of action who obey commands *instantly*.'

Two days later the bank was visited by a tough number with a head stocking and wielding a heavy revolver. 'Stick 'em up! Hand over all the money in the safe,' snarled the toughie.

The banker shouted to the detective, 'Let him have it! *Let him have it!*'

So the detective did.

* * *

Dermot thinks that Punk Rock is a penal island reserved for Irish criminals. And unoccupied because there aren't any.

* * *

The boss of a big Irish company worried about falling trade. He hired an expert to pin-point reasons for low figures. The expert made a thorough check right through the company, interviewing all the staff. Finally the Managing Director asked him for the verdict. The expert said, 'Come with me to the boardroom.' They went. There was a wall-map scarred by pin-pricks of agent's and rep's flags. 'My job's finished,' said the expert, 'and it will cost you £20,000.'

The boss said, 'I can see that some very elaborate and expensive re-assessment is going to be needed. You've earned your fees, but how many more thousands is this going to cost?'

'Not a cent,' said the expert, pocketing his fee, in cash. 'All you have to do is hike those pins outa the damned *wall* AND PROD 'EM IN THE BACKSIDES OF YOUR STAFF!'

* * *

Dermot said, 'Do you think it would be an insult if I paid you for the two rounds of drinks?'

Kelly said, 'I've always been a person not ashamed of swallowing an insult.'

* * *

Sheila was told to measure her husband's neck for collar size. She put her hands round and said, 'God give me strength.'

* * *

McDermot looked around the ballroom and said to Casey, 'I must be getting old. I'm finding more of the women looking attractive than this time last year.'

* * *

A young Irish girl walked into a lawyer's office and complained, 'My husband is a brute. I can't stand any more. I want to be rid of him, that I do.' The lawyer said, 'You mean a divorce?' Then because he wondered about her religion he added, 'Are you of a certain persuasion?' The young woman snapped, 'If you mean do I need encouragement, that depends on the feller.' The solicitor let it go and remarked, 'Has your husband given you grounds?' The girl said, 'You mean has he tried to poison me?'

'No,' said the lawyer, 'I mean has he done anything that would enable you to sue him for misconduct?' The girl said, 'Eh?' The lawyer simplified it by asking, 'I mean, using the colloquial, has he been having a bit on the side?'

'I don't know,' she answered, 'and if he uses a colloquial that's news to me.' The lawyer said, 'If he hasn't given you grounds for a divorce and you want to be rid of him, you could let him divorce *you*, you know, by giving him grounds to part from you.'

'I see,' said the girl. 'But won't that cost a lot of money.' Helpfully the solicitor explained, 'Well, in your particular case, considering your financial position, *you* could get legal aid.' The girl thought for a moment and then said, 'Well, all right, if you're not too busy, but it will have to be around half past ten on Friday night so that he can catch us properly.'

*   *   *

Shamus told the dentist as he sat in the torture chair: 'And let me tell you dis from de start, if you make a mess of me mouth I'll be demandin' me teeth back.'

*   .*   *

Two Irish Friars were walking along the main road when they came across a dowdy old woman crying her eyes out. One of the friars asked her what ailed her. 'I've been sacked from me job,' she wailed. 'Where were you working?' inquired the second friar. 'I 'ad a good job as an attendant in the Ladies',' the old woman answered. So the first friar inquired, 'But why did they give you the sack?' The old lady sobbed, 'I couldn't remember the prices.'

* * *

Last week the Unemployment Figures were up again, I see. Over 650,000 people were out of work. Mind you 300,000 of them were just on strike.

* * *

An errant husband returned home blind stinko at three a.m. in the night, crept as quietly as possible into the bedroom and held his alcoholic breath when his wife stirred in her sleep, turned and murmured, 'Is that you, Fido?' What he did was bend down quickly and lick her arm.

* * *

O'Neill told his wife, 'I've taken out a double-indemnity policy. I took it out without understanding what it was. The insurance man told me . . . When I die, they bury me twice.'

* * *

The Vicar of Clareol states that the secret of tranquillity of mind is to be happy with your lot. Presumably no matter what a rotten lot your lot are.

*   *   *

The new bride was preparing herself for bed in the honeymoon suite when she muttered, 'Moike, know something?'
'What,' he inquired breathlessly. 'Well,' she said, 'I think they've redecorated this room since I was last here.'

*   *   *

Strokes of Irish Genius. He spent three weeks trying to invent a new style shoulder-strap for topless dresses.

*   *   *

Early marriages among students have created fresh problems for some Irish universities. A new college in the north has half solved the problem by issuing an edict. From now on married girls must either live with their husbands or else make other arrangements with the caretaker.

*   *   *

The three best things in life are a whisky before and a cigarette after. Or better still – poteen.

*   *   *

Ulster Television has announced another series of repeated series for next summer. It is such a full programme of repeats that 'Gardening Club' will devote the whole half-hour to growing radishes.

* * *

My wife is just like a two-year-old. Not horse. Egg.
                    Says Irish Comic Neil O'Malley

* * *

Paddy was telling his cronies in the pub about his firstborn: 'And that night she was having the baby, she yelled and screamed and fought and kicked and struggled and shrieked and squirmed. All hell was let loose. It was terrible to watch . . . and I wouldn't mind, but that was only when she conceived.'

* * *

Did you hear about the Irish angler, Kim, who made a new net two miles wide and eight miles long? He forgot how to cast off.

* * *

O'Riley went to the classified advertisement department of his local newspaper to write out an advertisement announcing the birth of his baby son. The clerk checked the announcement and asked the customer, 'How many insertions?' The customer snapped, 'Don't get personal!'

* * *

Shaun is a staunch trade-unionist, a shop-steward and convenor. Last night I had to pop in there to give him a message and he said, 'Wait a minute, I'm just telling the kids a good-night bedtime story . . .' And then I heard him begin the story of Cinderella. 'Once upon a time-and-a-half Cinderella was staging a sit-down strike in front of the fire in the Capitalist-swine Baron's castle . . .'

* * *

Two Martian youngsters met at a discoteque and the young male Martian was very attracted to the young female Martian. So, as was the custom, they went together. Afterwards the male one said, 'By the way, I'm BM 2331. What do they call you?' The female one said, 'I'm YDS 324.'
'That's strange,' said the male. 'You don't *look* Irish.'

* * *

In a nightclub one night, Paddy ordered chicken and when the waiter brought his meal, he looked at the plate and said, 'Look, you've given me a chicken with only one leg!' The waiter gesticulated and said, 'I thought you wanted to eat it, not dance with it.'

* * *

The foreman was astonished to find one Irish road-maker with TWO SPADES IN HIS HANDS! – and three clubs.

* * *

81

Patrick had the problem of trying to tell his six-year-old son that his wife was expecting another child. He sat Sean on his knee and said awkwardly, 'Look. Sean, in a few days time, a big beautiful stork is going to come flying right over our house, flapping his mighty wings, and he'll make a three-point landing on our roof and drop a big package of joy straight down our chimney – a special gift from Heaven!' Sean pulled a face and said, 'I hope the stupid bird doesn't frighten the daylights out of Mom – didn't *you* know she was pregnant again?'

*　　*　　*

Clodagh was applying to the court for a divorce. 'What were your relationships with your husband like?' asked the judge. 'Diabolical,' she said. 'Was he a friendly man?' asked the judge. 'Look,' she said, 'in the four years of our marriage he only ever spoke to me three times.' The judge went back over the evidence in front of him, then shrugged and said, 'Divorce granted. And I give you the custody of the three children.'

*　　*　　*

'What happened just now, McGraw? What was that scuffle on the corner of the lane?'
'It was nutting at all, at all, constable. I was just instrumental in saving two young ladies from being attacked.'
'Did you, bejabers! And how did you manage that?'
'When I saw you coming I changed my mind and let 'em go.'

*　　*　　*

The Judge, during a brawling case, was requestioning the defendant, a rather stocky, muscular Irish gent. 'Tell me again,' said the Judge, 'exactly what happened when you took this – er – female companion into the cabin of the cargo boat.' The man said, 'Like I told ye, we went into the ——ing cabin, turned on the ——ing light, had a couple of ——ing whiskies, and then she got kind of ——ing awkward, and —— me if she didn't start chucking ——ing things around, so I grabbed her to knock some ——ing sense into her and, well, somehow we fell on the floor, and before I knew it, if you'll pardon the expression, your Honour – we indulged in intercourse.'

*   *   *

'Well,' said the doctor sternly, 'what's wrong with you, young man?'
'I got my finger stuck in a zip.' The doctor said, 'Does it hurt?' Paddy said, 'Not much, but I can't keep dragging this girl along everywhere I go.'

*   *   *

There's a tall new apartment block in Liverpool where the slum areas have been cleared. One day Sean came home from work, walking up the three thousand stairs to the twelfth floor because the kids of the neighbourhood had sabotaged the lifts by blowing the doors off. He went into his flat and said to his wife, 'There's a rumour going around the building that the postman has had affairs with every damn woman in this place except one.' His wife said nastily, 'I bet it's that rotten stuck-up floozie Mrs Wilkins on the fifth floor.'

*   *   *

Paddy went into the office and left his wife outside. Four minutes later he came out very angry, and snorted, 'Imagine that! Calls himself a taxidermist and can't even cure me ingrowing big-toe!'

*　　*　　*

On a farm in Co. Clare there is a world-famous bull named Oscar who cost over forty-thousand pounds and who is in much demand by cattle breeders all over the county. One fine morning a middle-aged man called at the farm to see the farmer and he was invited into the house by the farmer's wife. 'I want to see your husband,' said the stranger. The wife said, 'If it's about the bull, I can deal with it . . .' The man said, 'I'd rather speak to your husband; the matter is very delicate.' She said, 'It's all right. You can talk to me, I know how much he charges.' The man said, 'I'd rather talk to your husband.' The farmer's wife said, 'Look, if it's about the bull, I know all the facts and figures . . .' The man said angrily, 'It's nothing to do with the bull. I want to talk to your husband about your swine of a son – he's been carrying on with my young daughter and now she's in trouble . . .' The farmer's wife said, 'Oh. Then wait a minute. I'll have to call my husband. I don't know how much he charges for our Peadar!'

*　　*　　*

Drunk as two sailors Murphy and Pat returned to their Belfast hotel when they paused to listen. Inside the room the man was saying to his bride, 'Avril, you are so deliciously lovely, your fabulous beauty ought to be captured for posterity by the best artist in the world!' The two drunks banged on the door immediately, and the husband shouted, 'Yes, who is it?' The men answered, 'It's Reubens and Rembrandt!'

* * *

A Kerry headmaster received a note from an angry parent. 'I'm extremely concerned about my son's report which I have just received. Not only has he got very low marks in all subjects, but he left school three years ago!'

* * *

Statistics state that during a normal day a bus-conductor will walk twenty six miles. Why doesn't he catch a bus asks a reader?

* * *

Regan won £50,000 on the pools, so they couldn't very well refuse his subscription when he wanted to join the golf club. All they can do is look the other way as he spits on his hands before wielding his mashie.

* * *

Are you a regular churchgoer, O'Hara?'
None better, vicar. I go every Easter.'

* * *

A tourist stopped his Range Rover at the brow of the frighteningly steep hill that dropped half a mile into the sleepy village of Finbarr. 'Excuse me,' the driver said, button-holing an obvious local native, 'but isn't it very dangerous in this area?' The local said, 'Well, it's not too bad up *here*, but nobody walks away from the accidents at the bottom!'

*　　*　　*

While he was in the USA an Irish farmer became aware of progress, and so ordered a wind generator to be installed on his place back home. Immediately his neighbour Clancy saw this invention and he ordered a wind generator for his adjoining farm. The other man complained and ordered Clancy to take it down again because there wouldn't be sufficient wind for both.

*　　*　　*

'Want to buy a lottery ticket for a poor needy widow woman, Liam?'
'Likely not,' said Liam, 'what'd I do with her if I won her?'

*　　*　　*

Three cousins were moving furniture to help an uncle change house. Liam and Casey both were perspiring with the effort. 'Where's Francis? I've not seen him since we dropped the mirror,' said Liam. Casey said, 'Oh stop mithering. He's right with us, holding the hangers in this wardrobe.'

*　　*　　*

Mrs McManus was annoyed when her little lad kept rushing in and out scoffing apples. She caught him on the seventh circuit – she grabbed his braces and shouted, 'Now that's enough apples . . . they don't grow on trees, y'know!'

*　　*　　*

'Excuse me farmer,' said the Irish farm-hand, 'but did you know that your wife has been chased around the hayrick by the new bull for over an hour?'
The farmer roared, 'You dolt, why didn't you say so earlier?'
'Why?' asked the lad. 'Does she get tired quickly?'

*　　*　　*

The first week they were married Shaun gave all his money to Dana and only kept £1 for himself. Dana said in surprise, 'Eeee!' On the following payday Dana said, 'I don't know how you managed on £1, especially with lemonade at 50p a glass. I don't understand how you do it!' Shaun said, 'You'll bloody know, me darlint – *it's your* turn for the pound this week.'

*　　*　　*

The owner of the horse entered at the Curragh was disappointed with its performance. He scolded his jockey very severely. 'You ought to have gone a whole lot faster over the last ten furlongs.' The rider said, 'I know that, boss, but I had to stay back with the horse.'

*　　*　　*

Sean said that his Irish ancestry went back to the Ark. O'Neal claimed that his family was even older because his ancestors had all worked on the docks where the Ark was built. Sean said, 'The hell they did! My family back to Noah's day remember your mob went on strike every time there was a shower.'

* * *

An Irish brickie fell forty feet on to a pile of rubble. 'Get him some water,' shouted the foreman. 'He's unconscious.' The brickie raised himself up and snorted, 'How many bloody feet do you have to fall to get a shot of brandy in this crummy mob!'

* * *

Mrs Clancey took her husband Pete to consult the psychiatrist and said, 'We all know it's a lot of malarky, him thinking he's a hen – but while we're here, can you do anything about his fowl pest?'

* * *

Jamey went with his pal to the hospital to visit their mutual friend. When they got there the doctor told them that their friend had just passed away. Jamey asked the cause and the doctor said, 'My memory isn't too good these days, and I can't remember, but I don't think it was anything serious.'

* * *

She said to Dermot, 'Dinner will be late. It's *boeuf braise aux carottes et pommes en province via Tesco* in a handy pack, but I've had to send to Dieppe for a cylinder of French gas.'

*   *   *

Kelly was being interviewed by the affluent father of his girlfriend Liandra. 'Well, what are your prospects in life, me bhoy?'
The swain paused, then said, 'Very, very good, sor.' Then as an afterthought he added, 'granted your little lass didn't seriously mislead me, your honour, sor.'

*   *   *

When a colleen says she won't be a moment, she's usually right. It could be an hour.

*   *   *

Cassidy ordered a television set and required the goods on credit. The salesman asked him, 'Can you produce some references, sor, if you don't mind accommodating the company?' Cassidy smiled broadly and said, 'But for sure! Faith, won't the dealer where I got me last model from assure you that there was not a single scratch on the cabinet when he took it back!'

*   *   *

'I've come to sign on.'
'You've come to sign on what?'
'Would it be de dotted line, sor?'

*   *   *

Flavin and his wife were watching a local football match and the rain was pelting down in sheets, soaking the fans on the open terraces. The wife said, 'Look Mike, I know I'm innocent of the finer aspects of the game, but would you mind if I asked you a question?' 'Sure, Blodwin,' smiled her husband, 'it's a pleasure to see you so interested. What would you have me explain?' Blodwin said moistly, 'Why can't we bloody well go home?'

* * *

All the time that he was away from home, faithful young Mrs O'Grady kept a light burning in the window. And when he got back after eight years, they had to sell the house because they had an electricity bill for £17,450.

* * *

Young Cassidy had an evening off so he went to the fairground and took his girl through the tunnel of love. They came out soaking wet. Asked if the boat had sunk, he said, 'You mean there's a boat?'

* * *

The O'Hara family were on holiday by the sea and father was on the cliff-top, still wearing his pack. As the sea roared like fury 22,000 feet below, little Mike tugged his dad's anorak and said, 'Mamma says will you keep further away from the edge or else give me the sandwiches.'

* * *

In church on Sunday the vicar made a special appeal for funds to rebuild the church roof. When the plate came round, Phelan's mother-in-law put a Do-It-Yourself magazine on it.

* * *

O'Brian was being tried on charges of indecent assault, rape and driving without lights. His lawyer claimed that the rape charge was absurd. 'My Lord,' he said, 'the girl stopped my client's car on the highway with her leg, which she used to thumb a lift. And when my client drove on, the girl deliberately jumped into the back seat with him.'

* * *

O'Malley's boss took him to dinner to discuss a new contract. Afterwards the waiter brought the bill on the tray and the boss looked at it, pulled out his pretty purse, paid the exact sum and said to the waiter, 'Keep the tray.'

* * *

Shelagh went to the doctor because her chest and stomach ached, and after she'd prepared for the examination he said, 'And now, just tell me in your own words where I shall feel the pain.'

* * *

Soon there will be no more County Cork. The authorities are considering putting a stopper on it.

* * *

The Vicar of Galvin bought a talking parrot and taught it to say: 'And it shall come to pass that every sinner who remains a sinner shall surely go to hell.' The parrot finally got the sentence off pat. (Pat was the vicar's maid.) Anyway, one day the cleric decided to invite the bishop in for a brandy so that he could demonstrate his skill in religious matters. The bishop arrived. The parrot watched the two men imbibing Martell. Then the vicar introduced the parrot, and the parrot stared at the bishop and said, 'Go to hell . . . go to hell . . . go to . . .'

* * *

There was an Irish patrol fighting its way into Indo-China with tank and air support. One young officer was dangerously edging his way through the dense undergrowth when his walkie-talkie bleeped softly, almost drowned out by the heavy barrage going on. After listening for a minute, the lieutenant said, 'Of course I do, Rita. For Christ's sake, how many times have I told you not to ring me at work?'

* * *

A Belfast couple had been in bed in a suburban council house for three hours, enjoying all the mysteries of the darkness, when at two a.m. the bedroom door opened and another man walked in and started undressing as he said, 'I'm fed up with these identical council houses, lovey. I had trouble finding the dratted place again tonight – sorry I'm late!'

* * *

There was a big orgy in the Irish Railway Hotel and it got so unruly that the hotel manager had to send for a railwayman to come and unfasten the couplings.

* * *

O'Connor thinks that a booby-trap is a too-tight brassière.

* * *

A novice big-game hunter was on safari in the wilds, accompanied by half a dozen bearers, a guide and a white hunter. The girl fired at a moving target a thousand feet distant. There was a terrible roar. She said to the hunter, 'What do they call that beast I just shot?' The hunter said, 'The Bishop of M'Cree.'

* * *

One girl was on drugs and she got so high that Aer Lingus chartered a plane to get her down.

* * *

Dr O'Toole came out of the bedroom and told the wife, 'I don't much like the look of your husband.' 'Neither do I,' she admitted, 'but he idolizes the kids.'

* * *

Paddy says that the rudest Irish official is the one who has to look up women's particulars when they need money, and he's trying to get an extension of hours so that he can fit more in.

* * *

Brendon's psychiatrist discussed his problems with him and at the end he said, 'That was a very useful interview and I'll soon find out what makes you tick!' Brendon said, 'No, no. I know what makes me tick; I'm more worried about chiming the hours and half hours.'

* * *

O'Malley came home unexpectedly, having missed the train, and he surprised his wife entertaining the milkman. 'Here, here, what's the game!' he asked, with interest.
His wife said, 'I don't know what it's called, but it ought to catch on like a house on fire.'

* * *

When Brenda first got engaged her beau presented her with a massive one hundred carat diamond ring. She kissed him and swore, 'I shall treasure it truly and always, no matter who I marry.'

* * *

One morning James O'Hannigan awoke in great spirits and sang as he said, 'Wakey, wakey, wifey mine; today is the anniversary of our honeymoon, so let all be joy and laughter.'
'Oh Christ,' moaned his plump spouse, 'Have we got to go through all that again!'

* * *

Mike O'Casey had been a master bricklayer since childhood and had gradually needed more visits to his GP. He was examined again in the surgery. 'You need a course of injections,' said the doc, and proceeded to tinker about in his cubby-hole. 'What are you mixing in that tube?' asked O'Casey. 'Oh, the usual for your particular complaint – two sand and one of cement!'

* * *

Bill McCourt had had tough luck all through life. His marriage turned out to be a failure, too, so he decided to consult the experts at the marriage guidance centre. He almost got knocked down crossing the road, he tripped over three stairs going to the office: and when he gets there, whose managing the office? His mother-in-law.

* * *

It happened at the Irish Sessions Court.
The prisoner was being tried for attempted rape. The judge listened to all the evidence and said, 'For the offence you committed the sentence should be ten years in jail. But I'm going to be lenient with you. Fined five pounds.' Afterwards the clerk asked the judge why he had been so lenient considering the magnitude of the crime. The judge said, 'I've always believed in giving a man a second chance.'

* * *

'Do you understand German?'
'Shure I do if it's in an Irish accent.'

* * *

Mike McReady learned to fight hard when he was only in the third grade at school. That was the time the other kids saw the frilly lace gym shorts his mother had run up on her Singer.

*   *   *

Mike Flynn was fed up with the monotony of things, so one night he said, 'Come on, Nadia, let's try it a different way.' So they moved the bed away from the recess and put it opposite the fireplace.

*   *   *

What do they call a busy Irish carpet-fitter who is short of blood? Anaemic.

*   *   *

Mick was in good spirits throughout the journey until he fell out of the 'plane, singing: 'The song is ended but AER Lingus on.'

*   *   *

Paddy got a sectional bookcase. Then he put on his white raincoat and went to Soho to stock the shelves.

*   *   *

Paddy invented a special gadget for judges to use at seaside Beauty Contests. It's a breasterlyser.

*   *   *

Irish boxer Tim O'Connor was knocked out so often towards the end of his career that his manager started selling advertising space on his back in the ring.

* * *

What does an Irishman call a group of four people? An awesome.

* * *

Shaun thinks a drug addict is an assistant who counts out the pills for a busy pharmacist.

* * *

Then there's the Irish vampire who only drank Bloody Marys.

* * *

O'Hara got his indenture and had it framed to exhibit in his office, but all his clients thought he was an extractor of teeth.

* * *

Irish songstress Celia is so thick-skinned her 38 bust takes a 40 cup bra.

* * *

Her husband demanded, 'Is there another man, Clo-dah?' And she said, 'No, 'course not. Only you and Pat and Oscar and Eamonn as always.'

*   *   *

A Scot thinks twice before he speaks; an Englander thinks once before he speaks; and an Irishman doesn't have time to think even if he could.

*   *   *

Typical tombstone in driveway of an Irish cemetery: 'This gravestone is erected in memory of Nick O'Rourke who was accidentally stabbed to death, as a token of abiding infection by his everloving wife.'

*   *   *

Donavon has just taken Holy Orders. The priest wants him to deliver a dozen prayer books, a tin of pew polish, six hassocks and an anthem board, and put them on the slate pending the next collection.

*   *   *

The young couple were in the car, in the dark lane, driving slowly and Fiona said, 'Can you drive with one hand?' Pat said, 'Yes,' and his lungs beat fast. Fiona said, 'Can you come a bit closer to me?' He gulped and said, 'Oh, yes!' She said, 'Well I've got an apple, have a bite.'

*   *   *

Young widow Carey complained to the dairy that the young milkman on the early round disturbed her and woke her up. The dairy manager promised action. The woman said, 'I don't mind the noise, but I must protest about the way his crate tears the bedsheets.'

*　　*　　*

An Irishman called for his dog. But even that wouldn't go out with him!

*　　*　　*

On any Irish air-strip even the searchlights are dim. They point downwards.

*　　*　　*

When Paddy prepared to take his driving test, he took the whole bag and three spare balls with him.

*　　*　　*

Paddy was so sick and tired of being the target for stupid jokes he changed his name by deed poll. To Mike.

*　　*　　*

Tim got lockjaw from taking his temperature with the wall barometer.

*　　*　　*

Phelen was riddled with bullets during a gang war in Manhattan. They never buried him. Because he had eighty bullets in him, the clan had him smelted.

*　　*　　*

The Belfast climate is so very, very healthy, says the handbook. In fact it puts years on you.

*　　*　　*

Kieran reckons he would rather die than be buried in an English cemetery.

*　　*　　*

Asked if he could add up a column of figures, Jason climbed the statue of the 'The Three Horsemen' and did his arithmetic up there.

*　　*　　*

Paddy was looking through the window of a vintners' where a wine expert was sampling a dozen in tests, and after he had spat out nine or ten glasses, Paddy said to his companion, 'You'd never get *me* in this pub, not for all the tea in Brazil.'

*　　*　　*

'How long have you *been* racing pigeons, Clusky.'
'Two months.'
'Why did you pack it in?'
'I fell off me kite.'

*　　*　　*

Paddy had never been in a gymnasium before and when he did visit one he saw an athlete doing push-ups with furious determination. Paddy watched for a while in confusion, then finally tapped the athlete on the head and said, 'Excuse me, sor, but I think your girl went, some time ago.'

*　　*　　*

There is this spurious wrestling organization in Ballywick where the referee shouts to the two maulers: 'That's the rules, and now back to your corners and come out acting.'

*　　*　　*

Passenger: 'Hey, watch out, he's driving right at you!'
Paddy: 'Well, two can play at that game, you know. Hold tight.'

*　　*　　*

'Coming home this evening I saved twelve pence by running behind the bus,' bragged Mike.
His wife snapped, 'Ye gormless fool, why didn't you run behind a taxi; you'd have saved £1.45!'

*　　*　　*

Shaun shouted over the fence, 'Fancy a game of Badminton?'
Casey called back, 'There's no sense wasting time – ask me again when've improved a bit.'

*　　*　　*

The tinker was in court again. The judge said, 'If I'm not mistaken you came up three years ago in this very court for the same offence of stealing a pair of wellingtons!' Said the tinker, 'Well just listen to the man! How long does he think a pair of wellies lasts?'

* * *

A crafty Irish pickpocket beat the Court with an original excuse. He told the judge that he'd been told the average family in Belfast consisted of 3.4 people and consequently he wasn't all there.

* * *

His mother was very careful with baby Shaun. She used to dip him into a tub of hot water to see if it was fit for her to wash her arms.

* * *

The vicar concluded the Irish marriage ceremony . . . 'I now pronounce you man and nag.'

* * *

Caley's wife turned to her husband and said, 'Take that tie off, it clashes with the curtains.'

* * *

The most popular meal to get from the Irish Take-Away café?
Irish Stew-in-a-Basket.

* * *

Casey fell down the pub steps after a long session. Both his legs were broken. At the hospital the surgeon examined him minutely and then assured him: 'Don't worry about a thing, within eight weeks of amputating your legs I'll have you back on your feet.'

* * *

Paddy can remember when a late shift was an antique chemise.

* * *

Phelen the suitor said to the girl's father, 'Oi'd be having the honour to marry your pretty lady daughter, sor. If you have the room, dat is.'

* * *

Mullarkey and his wife have been holding hands for seven years. If they were to let go they'd murder each other.

* * *

An Irish crook took the afternoon off to go to the cinema, but he didn't like the film so he went to the cashier and demanded his money back . . . *and everyone else's.*

* * *

Mulligan was watching through the window where a pansy was taking infinite pains to produce an elaborate hair-style for a beautiful Irish girl. 'Hell's bells,' he muttered, 'would you just look at that shinanagin'! Sure an' it's enough to curl your hair.'

* * *

Finnigan went to the store to buy a colour TV set and the salesman was a sour old lad. Finnigan asked the price of one of the models, and the salesman said, 'Can't you read? It's on the ticket right there in black and white!' Finnigan shouted, 'You old fool, didn't I ask you for a colour one!'

* * *

Mike's wife was a highly suspicious and jealous woman. Whenever he got home, she immediately scoured him, searching for foreign female hairs, and if she found one she went into violent recriminations. One night she searched him and he was as clean as a whistle. In bitter tears she shouted, 'So now it's even *bald* women!'

* * *

Sheila said, 'For years I kept wondering where my husband was all the time, then one night I went home from the pub and there he was!'

* * *

'Classical music,' says Killian, 'is when you put on a record and it takes forty minutes for the tune to come round.'

*   *   *

Patrick explains history. Says he, 'The Romans made their roads dead straight to prevent the English from hiding round corners!'

*   *   *

An Englishman came in for a shave and Finigan the barber was busy. His small son, ten-year-old Brendan said, 'I could shave the gent, Dad, if he's in a hurry.' The barber said, 'Well have a go if you like, but mind you don't cut yourself.'

*   *   *

O'Malley remembers his wedding day well. So does his wife. He never worked again after he carried her over the threshold.

*   *   *

Poor old Kelly. He decided to drown his troubles in drink and discovered they were naturally buoyant.

*   *   *

'Sure,' said Mike, 'here in Ireland we could have the best weather there is anywhere in the world if the climate didn't spoil it.'

*   *   *

An old stage friend met Clancy after many years and asked, 'What happened to that beautiful show-girl who was your partner in the magician's act at the Empire? The one you used to saw in half twice nightly.' Clancy said, 'Oh she's still around. She lives in Wales now – partly in Rhyl and half in Prestatyn.'

* * *

The boss asked Kelly, 'Do you have a flair for figures?'
'Indade I do, sor,' said Kelly.
'Then get upstairs and burn the books – the revenue men are coming.'

* * *

Returning from holiday O'Hagen said, 'We've had a fortnight on the sand. Now we'll be a month on the rocks.'

* * *

'What's your new home like, Finigan?'
'Not too bad. But the bedroom's very small and every time I open the door a light comes on.'

* * *

Hannigan tried to stand on his head in the gymnasium, but he found that he couldn't get his legs up high enough.

* * *

An Irishman complained that some vandal had thrown a dead rat through his dining-room window and broken a glass cabinet. The Irish detective told him, 'If nobody claims the animal within three months, it's yours.'

*   *   *

Gamewarden in Irish Park sees young lad fishing in the ornamental pond and warns him, 'You are not allowed to fish in these waters, you little spalpeen.' 'Who the heck's fishing? I'm just teaching my little pet worm to swim!'

*   *   *

Asked what his previous job was, Paddy explained he was a self-employed Security Officer who fitted combination locks on garbage cans.

*   *   *

To keep up the festive spirit Mike went out and bought his wife some holly for Whitsun.

*   *   *

Liam could not afford to buy his lad a yo-yo. He only managed to get him a yo.

*   *   *

Duffy placed an announcement in the local paper to report that he had found the watch he lost the previous week.

*   *   *

Paddy had an accident moving the piano. He fell off the keyboard. Fortunately, he explained, he hit the soft pedal.

*   *   *

O'Toole went all the way to France to see an exciting leg-show. It turned out to be the Six-Day Cycle Race.

*   *   *

Rafferty was in great trouble with flat feet. Some woman complained to the police that he trespassed there after midnight.

*   *   *

An Irishman who bought a pub was annoyed when he served his first customer. He told the assistant barman, 'Will you look at that! My first customer and he leaves me a 50p tip and doesn't pay for his beer!'

*   *   *

Hennesey regarded Paddy's second-hand wreck in astonishment as it squealed to a halt. Said he, 'It's a long time since you played with your *first* rattle, ain't it, Sterling?'

*   *   *

An Irish hobo called at a farmhouse and begged the lady, 'Please could you manage a small crust?' She gave him a slice of Hovis. The next three days, too, he went to the house and asked for a crust.

On the fifth day he knocked and asked, 'Would you be having a crumb or two of iced cake left over? Today's me birthday.'

*　　*　　*

An Irishman used to sing for his supper and the publican gave him a few pennies and a pint for each rendering. One evening a stranger visiting the village from America asked him, 'Would you like to have a go at 'Galway Bay' for twice what the landlord pays?' The Irishman looked embarrassed and ran out of the pub. 'Sorry about that, sir,' the landlord said to the Yank, 'he's very shy about strangers.'

And about two hours later the Irishman walked into the pub, wringing wet, and said, 'I tried my best but the bay's so stormy tonight I could only manage half way and had to turn back.'

*　　*　　*

Did you hear about the Irish steel industrialist who was so absent-minded he took his wife to dinner instead of his secretary?

*　　*　　*

O'Neil was a scratch golfer so his wife thought she'd knit him a hair-shirt and now he's had to join a monastery.

*　　*　　*

O'Henty thinks that a toadstool is a stool which has toes.

* * *

The conductor shouted, 'Move farther down the car please.' So Paddy pushed his dad into a corner.

* * *

A reporter on a county paper in Ireland printed a long article about a local dairyman who had made an immense fortune by short-measuring the housewives' and price-fixing cream. The article concluded: 'He owes his whole crooked fortune to udders.'

* * *

Belfast police are trying to stop gambling, but it seems to have got a grip on them.

* * *

After a magnificent dinner prepared by a titled Irish Lady at her imposing chateau the butler announced, 'Will you please now take coffee in the library.' Shaun O'Malley, who had been a last-minute substitute for an invalid footman shouted, 'You must be joking! De bloody library closes at five o'clock in dis god-awful villidge.'

* * *

Maloney tried desperately to give up the booze, but in the end demon drink conquered him and all he could do was keep getting his knees soled and heeled.

* * *

'Shure there's no denying the fact, green vegetables is the lifeblood of the body. Did yez ever see a rabbit wearing bifocals or taking the medicals?' said Shamus.

* * *

Hannigan was living the life of O'Riley, and then O'Riley skipped over the wall and returned home unexpectedly. That night there was the wearing of the green followed by the drawing of the blood.

* * *

Mrs O'Toole shouted out to her lad who was siting on the grass reading a comic paper, 'What are you doing out there in that pouring rain, Dermot?'
'Gettin' soaking wet, ma.'

* * *

Flattery always insisted that in schooldays the mistress Dana had a secret passion for him, on the evidence that she filled his exercise books with scores of crosses.

* * *

Casey was an old newspaper vendor who hardly made a bare living. Very few Irish readers wanted to buy old newspapers.

*   *   *

'I've been paying my psychiatrist £5 an hour to examine my mind,' admitted Shamus to his closer friends, 'and it hasn't done very much good for me.'
'So what can you do?' asked Kelly.
'I'm gonna ask for my mania back,' said Shamus.

*   *   *

Behan was trying to sell his mare in order to raise funds for a donation to the brewery.
'Are you sure she's thoroughbred?' he was asked.
'Positively.'
'And can the animal jump?'
'Like a bird, sir, I'm telling you,' insisted Behan, and added desperately, 'Jump! Look-it, I have to give notice to local air-traffic controllers whenever this rare beast is scheduled in a race.'

*   *   *

It's a shame about the lies competitors claim against the small-time builder O'Conor. One man keeps insisting that O'Conor gave Ireland a bad record when he built that tower in Pisa. What with it being so near the Vatican.

*   *   *

What do they call a pregnant Irishwoman? A dope carrier.

* * *

What do they call an Irish trainer pacing his champion on a bicycle? A dope peddlar.

* * *

How can you recognize an Irish crossbreed? By his striped trews, tartan donkey jacket and Hush Puppy wellies.

* * *

An Irishman invented a new type of parachute which opens on impact.

* * *

Then there's the Irish Sea Scout who went camping and his tent sank.

* * *

Have you seen an Irish Firing Squad? They form a circle . . .

* * *

Then there's the Irish tap-dancer found dead in a sink.

* * *

Paddy is now writing his memoirs as a Kamikazi rear-gunner.

* * *

The Irish terrorists last night demanded a ransom of 1 million French pounds and two parachutes before agreeing to return the hi-jacked submarine.

* * *

The weedy Paddy was being examined by the doctor. He asked him, 'How long is it since you had intercourse?' The patient thought, then said, 'It must have been around 1915.' The doctor said: 'That's an awful long time to go denying yourself a perfectly normal practice.' The patient said: 'I don't know, doc, according to your clock it's only 19-40 now.'

* * *

An Irish company gave its entire staff a day off to go to the local zoo. Shortly after the group arrived one of the visitors was in difficulty in the ornamental lake. He shouted loudly, 'One of the bleedin' crocodiles has snapped off one of me legs!' The works convenor asked, 'Which one?' and the victim yelled, 'They all look alike, you old fool.'

* * *

Thieves escaped with £560,000 from a Belfast banking establishment late last night. The Belfast police are trying to fathom out the motive.

* * *

O'Leary worked as a glassblower and after hitting the bottle during the lunch break, he had a troublesome bout of hiccups when he resumed work, and before anyone could help he'd blown 187 beer mugs.

*　　*　　*

The farmer's wife asked why he had been so late getting back from the fields and Patrick explained, 'I met up with the parson while I wus driving the mules, and from then on the poor critters couldn't understand a word I said.'

*　　*　　*

Shaun was very worried and his darlin' wife told him, 'I don't loike seeing you loike this. Your troubles is my troubles, so we'll mither it out together.'
'Roight,' says Shaun, 'I've had me a letter from dis girl in Dundalk and she's suing me and you for breach of promise, with an affiliation order on the soide.'

*　　*　　*

'What kind of fool are you, O'Malley! Trying to play checkers wid a pussy cat!'
'Well de pussycat's no fool, he beat me the last three games.'

*　　*　　*

An Irish specialist has perfected a method for women to get slimmer without special diets. He sews up threequarters of their stomach.

*　　*　　*

'The boss told me this afternoon, "Flattery will get you nowhere." '
'That's very true, daughter. Heed his wise words.'
'Rubbish, mother . . . He already owns three restaurants and wants me to become "*Mrs* Flattery."'

*　　*　　*

Ireland is enjoying a boom in tourism. There have never been so many millionaires in Shamrock Country – most of them waiters.

*　　*　　*

Little Irish Terror: 'Grandpa, was you wiv Noah in the Ark?'
Granpa: 'Well, I can't say I was, to be honest.'
L.I.T.: 'Then how come you wasn't drownded?'

*　　*　　*

'O'Hennessey,' said the judge, 'I am going to give you a suspended sentence.'
'Tanks, your highness, I'm obliged for your lenience.'
'All right, officers, take him out and hang him.'

*　　*　　*

'Did you like going to the Egyptian Room at the Art Gallery?'
'Indaid I did. And I also saw a great big advert for Elastoplast.'

*　　*　　*

Paddy announces the band's repertoire: 'And now the Irish Dixie Quintet will play a medley of five popular songs for you, "Three Coins in the Fountain" and "Two Sleepy People".'

*   *   *

O'Toole told his wife, 'I went into an auction room and got something for nodding. And all it cost me was £6,' he added.

*   *   *

Mulligan had the Seven Year Itch. Until a friendly chemist gave him something for it. £1.50.

*   *   *

'Mom, can I go and see the Aurora Borealis.'
'All right, Patrick, but don't get close; you hear!'

*   *   *

Shamus started on the bottom rung of the ladder, and is now fifteen inches into the ground.

*   *   *

He thinks that the orderly who puts the hypodermic syringe into a patient's backside at an army hospital was trained as a rear gunner.

*   *   *

An Irishman managed to get a job with the Gas Board and was told to read meters, so he hustled slowly to the Public Library.

*   *   *

Kelly opened a new restaurant and put up an attractive sign: 'Same-Day Service Guaranteed'.

*   *   *

Kelly went into town and bought a smoking jacket. He didn't know it was smoking until the cigarette end dropped.

*   *   *

Kelly races pigeons. And on only one occasion has he come in first.

*   *   *

Definition of an Irish Shakespearian Thespian. Tall, dark and some ham.

*   *   *

Kelly saw a sign outside a shop reading, 'Clothes to Rent', so he went in and slashed a few.

*   *   *

Kelly bought a typewriter. It took him six hours to write a letter. At that rate he'd need 24 hours to write a 4-letter word.

* * *

Kelly walks twenty miles when he goes shopping. He could do it all locally in ten minutes but he's determined to make his money go further.

* * *

Kelly advertised for a daily woman, and for the year he hired 365.

* * *

Kelly has designs on a number of women. He's a tattooist.

* * *

Kelly went into an outfitter's and bought a half dozen topless vests, to take off at the gynasium.

* * *

Kelly became a burglar. He never stole anything but at least he was his own boss.

* * *

Kelly has invented a unique gadget for speeding things up in go-slow factories. It's called a whip.

* * *

There are only two known specimens of a Neanderthal idiot's head in historical archives. The British Museum has one of them and Kelly has the other.

*   *   *

Kelly the crook jumped on a victim one night, stuck his gun into the poor victim's stomach and hissed, 'One high-pitched scream' from you and I'll blow ye brains out.'

*   *   *

Kelly's lovely daughter was being picked up so often, her father fitted her with handles.

*   *   *

Shaun opened a Chinese restaurant and the food was so awful the flies used to eat next door.

*   *   *

Kelly had a good meal of patterned paper, vinyl paint and minced plaster. He's training to be an interior decorator.

*   *   *

In 1957 a man was cast away on a lonely Pacific island with only a sandy-haired junior for company . . . A naval nurse.

*   *   *

Kelly used to take his pigs to market religiously every Thursday but he never had any luck selling them. Maybe it's because Market Day was Monday . . .

*   *   *

Killikenny was a typical one-horse Irish town, but that's all changed now. The horse got fed up with it as well and moved to Patifinny.

*   *   *

A middle-aged Irishman kept getting married and divorced and remarried time and time again, because he liked wedding cake so much.

*   *   *

Paddy suffered from foot trouble for twelve years and it wasn't until he died that they discovered there was nothing wrong with him except he always had his boots on the wrong feet. He might have discovered the mistake earlier, but he was always too scared to go to the dentist.

*   *   *

Paddy invented a fifty-foot high milking-stool for making it easier to milk coconuts.

*   *   *

Paddy was knocked unconscious when someone struck him on the head with a full bottle of pop. Lucky for him it was a soft drink.

*   *   *

There was a bad gas leak in the kitchen, so Shaun put a bucket under it. 'You idiot,' snapped his old father, 'that's not going to help. Turn the electric off at the main before we all get drowned.'

*   *   -

None of them could drive a car properly. They couldn't get it started. Then Clancy noticed a plaque on the dashboard marked 'Push to Start'. So all six of them got out and pushed.

*   *   *

The Kennedy family is the only one that travelled from Ireland to America in the Mayflower. They alone had money for the fare.

*   *   *

They put on a show in Belfast last week and it was so rotten that the manager was refunding audiences' money as they entered, and some clients demanded compensation.

*   *   *

McClusky was crossing through an alley in the dark when a man jumped out of the shadows and snarled, 'Put 'em up!' in a strong Scottish accent. McCluskey said, 'Put *what* up?' The footpad snorted, 'Trust me to pick on a perishing Paddywhack!'

*   *   *

An Irish producer at the BBC received various complaints about cruelty, torture and neglect that he amended the programme and put on a war film.

*   *   *

The only thing that works normally at the motor factory now is the hooter. The place is deserted apart from Mike the caretaker. And if nobody claims it after fourteen days he could grab the lot. Fortunately he's daft enough to turn it over to Lost Property.

*   *   *

Moriarty worked as a part-time barman. Some snooty English visitor snapped at him, 'Give me a dry Martini, and hurry.' Moriarty thrust a dirty glass-towel at him and said, 'Dry your own and in future don't keep spilling your drinks all over.'

*   *   *

Paddy has a good steady job now. He talked himself into being the official RSPCA representative at wrestling bouts.

*   *   *